sunset craft books

Bonsai
Decorative Stitchery
Flower Arranging by Tat
Flower Preservation
Gifts You Can Make
Interior Art and Decoration
Pottery & Ceramic Sculpture
Sculpture with Simple Materials
Sunset Mosaics
Sunset Woodcarving Book
Things to Make for Children

Sunset mosaics

Sunset

mosaics

written and illustrated by

doris & diane lee aller

LANE BOOKS

MENLO PARK, CALIFORNIA

This book is designed by the authors. All mosaics included in it, with the exceptions as credited to Mr. and Mrs. Victor Naglik, Edith Hamlin, Mrs. Leland C. Bean and Mrs. Frederick Keast, were designed and made by the authors.

The photograph at the bottom of page 53 is the work of Miss Bonnie Ubing.

preface

This is another in a series of Sunset craft books by the talented and versatile Allers—a family that specializes in the gracious art of making beautiful and practical objects for use in the house and garden.

The work of Doris Aller has long been known to the readers of the craft columns in Sunset Magazine and to the followers of Sunset Books. She has written three Sunset craft books and collaborated on a fourth. Her books on woodcarving, leathercraft, and rug making have been well received in this country and abroad. The one on leathercraft was reprinted in England and translated into Norwegian. Her books were selected by the State Department for display at the United States exhibits in Warsaw and Moscow.

Co-author Diane has contributed projects and designs to her mother's other books. She studied mosaic in connection with her work for the degree of Doctor of Philosophy in art history.

The third member of this family, Paul, is a professional typographer. He designed the format for the series. Thanks to his talents, the woodcarving book was selected as one of the 50 Western Books of the Year when it was published.

It is the Allers' mission to inspire others to use their own talents to surround themselves with handmade objects of grace and beauty. We share their hope that this book may lead you to the pleasure of gracing your home with useful and decorative mosaics.

—EDITOR, *Sunset Books*

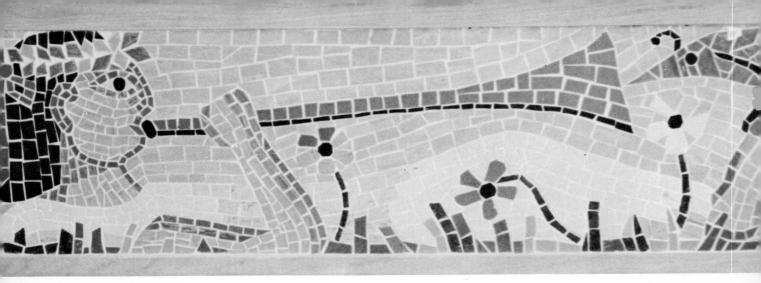

contents

	PAGE
INTRODUCTION TO MOSAIC	11
MOSAIC METHODS AND MATERIALS	19
Glass tiles	28
Smalti	30
Stained glass	32
Bottle glass	34
Ceramic tile	36
Broken pottery	38
Linoleum	40
Pebbles and stones	42
Marble	44
Wood	46
Seeds	48
COLOR AND DESIGN FOR MOSAICS	51
MOSAIC PROJECTS FOR THE HOUSE	61
MOSAIC PROJECTS FOR THE GARDEN	79
MOSAIC FOR CHILDREN	93
IN CONCLUSION	96

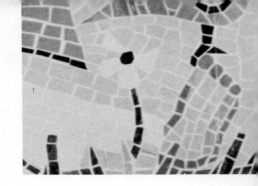

projects

Bread Board 63

TV Tray 64

Jack of Spades 65

Fruit Plate 66

Snack Board 67

Serving Tray 68

Harlequin 69

Quail 70

Owl and Pussy Cat 71

Plant Table 72

Towel Holders 73

Hi-Fi Cabinet 74

Occasional Table 75

Sea Gulls 76

Coffee Table 77

Compass Stone 81

Display Disk for Plants 82

Patio Table 83

Tile Squares 84

Wood Panel 86

Owl 87

Hanging Garden Ornament 88

Marine 89

Stepping Stones 90

Mosaic makes old surfaces new — ugly ones can be made beautiful. The first function of mosaic is to improve the qualities of a surface. Your first reason for making mosaic might be just because it is fun — and what better reason could one want . . .

introduction
to mosaic

This is a "how-to" book on mosaic. It will tell you how to make a mosaic, how to choose or make mosaic materials and where to use the mosaics you make. The techniques of mosaic making are thoroughly explored and special attention given to a wide range of mosaic materials.

During the course of its long history of use, mosaic has been done in many different materials, some as different from one another as eggshell and stone. Both of these, and many others, have been used. It isn't the material that identifies mosaic, however, but how the material is used. Choosing the right material is an important part of mosaic making because material often determines where and how certain mosaics can be used.

The prime function of mosaic is to improve the quality of a surface—any surface, large or small, from the façade of a building to the top of a jewel box. It may add beauty to an ugly surface or durability to a weak one. It often does both. A look at some of the high points in the history of mosaic shows how this function of mosaic has been used in the past.

Triangular pieces of red and black stone and white shell found in the ruins of a building at Ur suggest that Mesopotamian builders had already evolved a kind of mosaic in the third millennium B.C. It is very likely that bits of stone and shell were used to give a bright, protective coating to Mesopotamian wood, mud and reed architecture.

Floor surfaces, always a problem, were even more so in ancient times. Mosaic offered a good solution. A layer of small stones over a mud or stucco floor improved both its looks and its wearing qualities; it was also easy to do. Simple pebble mosaics of very high quality were made by the ancient Greeks. Several fine examples recently found in a third century B.C. building at Pella, Macedonia, show what can be done with natural materials if they are rigidly selected and carefully used.

To go on a bit with mosaic history, we find that small blocks of colored marbles were used for floors in Roman times. These blocks were probably scraps, left over from the manufacture of the great slabs of colored marbles that the Romans used to veneer their brick and concrete buildings. The value of these mosaics was more in their workmanship than in the material. Commonly, simple geometric designs were used, but more elaborate patterns, some even copying paintings, such as the *Alexander Mosaic* at Pompeii, were made too. In between these types were what we might now call "conversation piece" mosaics. A startling example of one of these is a mosaic floor which pictures the refuse of a Roman feast! The pattern even includes a mouse which has crept to nibble on the nut shells and fruit peelings presumably thrown down by the banqueters.

Later, mosaics were used to cover walls and the interiors of vaulted roofs as well as floors. Palaces and villas of Roman Emperors and early Christian churches were often decorated with vast expanses of mosaic which hid the plain building materials under a colorful, glittering surface. Glittering, because now mosaics were made of glass as well as marble. The glass was colored in jewel tones and some of it was fused with thin sheets of gold to make the mosaic bits look like chunks of solid gold. Mosaics of such materials were rich in appearance and very expensive to make, but churches decorated with them, such as Santa Sophia in Constantinople, have an other-worldly effect that could not be obtained in any other way.

Eventually, changing economic conditions stopped the widespread use of mosaic decoration. From the Renaissance to the present, however, mosaic has continued to be used on exterior walls since few other methods of surface decoration can equal its durable and decorative qualities.

Part of the pleasure of making mosaics today can be taken in the fact that one is continuing the use of an ancient art form. Mosaic making isn't merely an artificial revival of an ancient technique for its own sake by any means. It has a real use in modern life. We still need good looking, long wearing, easy-to-care-for surfaces. So the use of mosaic is just as valid today as it was in the third millennium B. C.

As valuable as mosaics may be in use, the present day popularity of mosaic making as a craft and hobby stems from the further fact that mosaic making is fun.

Mosaic making is quite easy to do, too. The technique is very simple. Small bits of material are used and the design worked out before they are placed. Each bit is a "tessera," which is Latin for square piece; the plural is "tesserae." The design, when it is drawn to the same size as the finished mosaic, is called a "cartoon." In the direct method, described later, the cartoon may be drawn on the surface being decorated and each tessera glued to it one at a time. Other methods involve more steps but are no more difficult. This makes mosaic making a highly satisfactory leisure-time activity — a pleasurable pastime. Especially as it is entirely possible for the beginner to make a successful mosaic at the first try. No need for a good idea to be spoiled by lack of experience, providing a few suggestions, given later, are followed.

All of the mosaic materials used in the past, from pebbles to the fused-glass golden tesserae are still available for us to use. New ones have been added and new glues and mortars make the ways of making mosaic even simpler.

As you begin to make mosaics you will find, as we did, that the people around you will want to try mosaic making too. Other members of the family, especially, will want to be included. If you want to make mosaics of pebbles or shells you'll surely have help in rounding up the materials. Families have made mosaics as a team, or the members join forces in some part of the mosaic making.

There are numerous worthwhile projects you will want to under-take. They needn't be large to qualify as worthwhile. Small accessories for the kitchen or table can be gay and quickly made. A neighbor of ours is making a dinner tray for each member of the family for the nights when they watch a favorite TV program.

Every house has furniture, floors and walls that can use some

This is a portrait of Schmeiner, Marie Bean's Weimeraner. Mrs. Bean did this mosaic picture of her dog in shades of grey and rust tile.

This antique earring is set with a mosaic made of minute bits of glass.

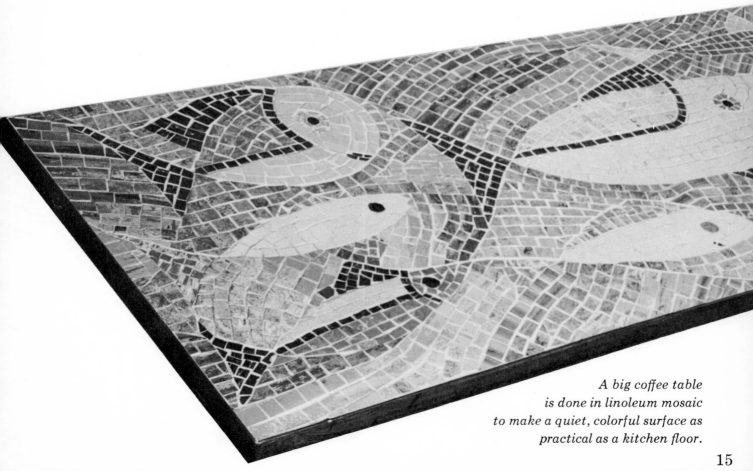

A big coffee table is done in linoleum mosaic to make a quiet, colorful surface as practical as a kitchen floor.

15

mosaic decoration. Many gardens will be enhanced with new stepping stones or other suitable outdoor decoration. There are many specific ideas in later chapters. There are also actual projects pictured and complete with patterns. You might make a start with any of them. They weren't included to make a copy-cat of you, necessarily, but to give you a starting place. To give you, too, ideas for things appropriately done in mosaic although those in this, or any book, couldn't exhaust all possibilities.

An excellent way to arrive at subjects for design motifs for mosaic decoration lies in examining some of your own close interests. It is a good way to "express yourself" through these interests, also. For instance, note the portrait included in this chapter. Mrs. Bean has created a picture in mosaic of her beautiful dog. She enjoyed the whole project and many others have taken pleasure in viewing the portrait.

If you want to make a mosaic as a gift, consider the special interests or hobbies of the person you want to give it to. We made the coffee table, also shown in this chapter, for a fisherman friend.

Will you need a studio, expensive tools and materials to make mosaic? No, none of these is essential however nice they might be to have. You will need a work table or bench of a good working height and a good light over it. We like to work out of doors whenever we can. If you work indoors with gritty materials, it is a good idea to spread a pad of newspapers on the floor around the work table. One of the tough paper "drop cloths" intended for room painting jobs makes clean-up especially easy.

As for expensive tools and materials, these hardly enter the picture in many mosaic projects. Cost is hardly a consideration when

The whole family helps put the finishing touches on this large mosaic panel. Mr. and Mrs. Victor Naglik made it for their future home. Their sons, Vic and Ric, share the grouting job.

you use pebbles, broken glass or crockery, scrap glass, tile or scrap pieces of linoleum. Even the cost of the imported glass tessera must be regarded as a small part of the value of the finished mosaic. Now, as in the past, the value of the mosaic lies in the workmanship, not the materials.

Make an outdoor ashtray by lining a big flower pot saucer with
mosaic. Just put a dab of ceramic tile setting mastic on the
back of a glass tile

and put it down. When bottom of the saucer
is covered with tiles, fill the cracks with a paste made of tile
setting grout and water.

mosaic methods
and materials

Pick up a small square tile, put a dab of mastic on the back, press it down on a dry surface—and you're on your way to making a mosaic. Few decorative treatments are simpler than making a mosaic by this direct method.

Instead of a tile, you might choose to stick down a pebble, a seed, or a little piece of colored linoleum. Modern mosaics are made of many things. Some of them can be bought—others must be sought. Special pages in this chapter will tell you where to look for, and find, eleven different materials for your mosaic making and ways to use them.

Besides the mosaic pieces, you'll need some glue or mortar to stick them down with and a suitable base to stick them on. Modern adhesives and mortars make it possible to put mosaic materials of many kinds on backings of metal, masonry, wood, sheet glass or plastic.

Plywood and other hard-surfaced composition boards are frequently used for mosaic backings and bases. Use these at least ¾″ thick for table tops and large panels. In most cases these plywood panels should be prepared for use by giving them a prime coat of shellac or waterseal.

If bases and backings are to be framed, have metal edgings, legs or hangers, attach these before setting the mosaic. To protect them from staining by glue or mortar, wrap or cover them well with masking tape.

Many outdoor projects have bases made of slabs of poured concrete. Don't dismiss working with concrete as being hard or heavy — we won't be working with contractor quantities. Several square feet of pebbles can be set in mortar equal to the amount of batter needed to make a layer cake. Like cake ingredients, it comes ready-mixed, too! You can buy big or little bags of dry-mix concrete and concrete mortar at building supply stores and at lumber yards. The concrete mix includes Portland cement, sand and rock or pebble aggregate. Concrete mortar is cement and sand.

If you want to make your own concrete mix, use one part Portland cement, two parts sand and three parts aggregate—this can be crushed rock or one of the lightweight aggregates such as Perlite, Haydite or Zonolite. Ask about these at builder supply stores and yards. Make cement mortar without the aggregate—just mix one part cement with three parts sand. Add water slowly when making up working batches of either concrete or mortar and use only enough to make a stiff paste.

A concrete bonding adhesive, sold where you buy the dry mix, makes extra-strong mortar. Mix two or three tablespoons of the bonding adhesive to each gallon of mixing water. To make a pebble setting paste for use on dry masonry, dilute this bonding adhesive half and half with water and then add enough pure Portland cement to make a buttery paste.

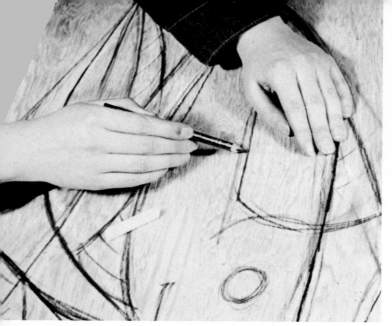

Plywood is good backing material for mosaics. Draw designs right on the clean wood surface. A coat of shellac keeps tracing lines clean and makes it easier to lift tesserae if you want to make changes. Lightweight plywood, ⅜″ or ½″ thick will do for small projects. Use ¾″ for table tops and large panels. For splash panels, and in those places where water will be present, use marine plywood or exterior grades of composition board. When you use glass or plastic sheet backing, shop for scratched or flawed pieces as these won't show in your finished work and flaws will reduce the price of such sheets.

Junk yards often provide good, inexpensive backings—an old refrigerator door will back an outdoor panel; a washing machine lid makes a good base for a birdbath.

Many good projects are refinishing jobs. An old tray takes on a new life with a mosaic lining. Make new tops on old tables, counters, benches. An ordinary box can become a treasure chest. Do prepare surfaces on old bases by filling any cracks or holes with patching compound, then sandpapering to smooth it down. Use sandpaper to rough up shiny varnished surfaces—sand shiny metal surfaces too.

Unfinished furniture sometimes presents surfaces that can be made distinguished with a mosaic. Give new wood on furniture two coats of shellac to minimize warping danger.

Concrete slabs used for bases of outdoor projects should be reinforced with hardware mesh if they are less than 4″ thick. Reinforced slabs may be as thin as 2″ if mesh is laid at one-half the depth. Cut mesh smaller all around by about 1″ so edges come well inside the block.

Always let concrete dry slowly and undisturbed. If mosaic pieces or pebbles are dislodged before concrete is well set they must be replaced with concrete bonding adhesive or they will not hold. Cover slabs with burlap and sprinkle with water once or twice a day for several days.

The favorite adhesive for setting tesserae on board backings is the now familiar "white glue." It comes in handy plastic "squeeze" bottles and jars, dries clear, is odorless and water-resistant. Clean up with water before glue is thoroughly dry.

Ceramic tile adhesive is quite water-resistant and you'll need thinner or lighter fluid for clean-up. It can be used for many mosaic materials and isn't limited to ceramic tile.

For transparent effects, such as gluing glass tesserae on glass backings or on plastic, use the clear household cement sold in tubes. You'll need acetone for clean-up.

Other materials, not thought of as adhesives, will nevertheless hold tesserae. One is the gun-metal colored body solder used in fender mending. Others are spackle, the common wall patching compound and other plaster and plastic mixtures. Small projects can have tesserae set directly in grout.

Grout is the fine-grained cement mortar used to fill cracks left between tesserae set with glue or ceramic tile adhesive. Buy it at mosaic supply stores, at tile setters and hardware stores.

Plastic resin doesn't qualify as either glue or mortar but acts more as a binding agent. It is a thick, syrupy liquid that sets hard and clear and it will hold mosaic pieces tight on bases or backings of sheet plastic. It is an exciting, challenging material to use for making translucent mosaics for use indoors or out. It is commonly sold for boat building and repairs and can be purchased by the quart or gallon at sports goods stores or plastic supply centers. The hardener or catalyst comes with it in a separate container and is added as you use the resin.

If you want to try a small experimental panel using plastics

Tile setting mastic can be used to set most mosaic materials on any dry base. It is especially useful for setting tesserae on vertical surfaces. Spread paste on backing or on backs of the tesserae. Because the thick mastic dries fast, take a small amount from the can and keep the rest tightly covered.

Milk-white casein glue is popular with mosaicists because it is odorless, dries fast and keeps well in the handy container. Brush it on or use the squeeze bottle to put drops of glue where you want them. If you are too generous with this glue it will cause the tesserae to float and they may raise or shift as the glue dries.

Grout, the fine white cement powder used for filling the cracks in mosaic surfaces is sold by the pint or pound. You'll need a pound of grout cement for every two to three square feet of mosaic surface you plan to grout. To mix grout, put a part of the dry powder in a clean bowl and add water a little at a time until you have a thick, creamy paste. If you get too much water, add some of your dry grout. Dry colors, available where grout is sold, can be added to dry grout to tint it.

Put a generous amount of the mixed grout on the face of your mosaic and spread it with hands or brush. Press it down into all the cracks. When surface is covered with the spread grout, remove the excess with soft cloths, a damp sponge or rubber spatula. Keep rubbing and clearing the surface until the grout is set.

When grout is completely dry, examine it for stray specks or spots of grout. Very fine steel wool will usually remove film—pick away specks with a steel point. Make the finished mosaic shine and waterproof the grout by coating it with silicone polish or liquid wax.

you'll need these things: a cup of resin, ½ teaspoon of catalyst, a rectangle of 3/16″ thick sheet plastic about 8″ x 10″, scrap glass in several colors and a roll of 1″ wide masking tape. Paper cups, stirring sticks can be thrown away—clean-up takes acetone.

Begin by sticking glass in desired arrangement to sheet plastic with clear household cement. Make a frame of masking tape around the sheet plastic at least ⅜″ deep. Use several layers of tape and press it firmly to edges and underneath to make frame leak-proof.

Set the rectangle of plastic with masking tape frame on a level place in the sunlight or under a heat lamp. Put syrup in the cup, add catalyst and stir thoroughly. Pour it over and around the glass to fill the rectangle. Plastic syrup will begin to gel in about twenty minutes. It will be hard enough for removal of the tape in about an hour. Don't pour plastic syrup indiscriminately over anything and everything—make a test first. It gives off heat as it sets and this sometimes breaks larger glass tesserae but the cracks do not mar decorative effects.

So far we have spoken of the many mosaic materials as used only by the direct method. You can always see exactly what you are doing in this way because tesserae are set right-side-up. They are glued directly to a backing or pushed into a bed of mortar. To get an even, level surface you must use materials such as tile, sheet glass or linoleum of all the same thickness if glued down. If pebbles or materials of different thicknesses are pushed into a mortar bed, take care to press them down evenly.

A flat surface is only important, however, on table tops, trays and counters. Pictures, wall panels, splash backs for outdoor foun-

Make a small panel for a beginning project in poured plastic. Choose a sunny day and work outside. Frame a sheet plastic backing with a masking tape frame to confine the liquid plastic syrup and arrange your colored glass pieces.

Put about a cup of the plastic resin in a paper cup and add about ½ teaspoon catalyst. Stir gently for a minute or two. Be sure your panel is sitting level, then pour the resin over and around the glass pieces.

Resin will start to gel in from fifteen to twenty minutes—should be hard enough so you can peel the tape from the edges in about an hour. After edges are thoroughly dry you can sandpaper them smooth and give them a further polishing with steel wool.

tains, birdbaths, etc., are more interesting with surfaces not flat or smooth.

Where a very flat surface is wanted, use what is called the "indirect" method. To do this, first reverse your design by turning it over and tracing it to a heavy sheet of brown paper. Use library paste or rubber cement and stick tesserae face down on the design. You will be able to see colors only if these show on both sides of your material.

When all the pieces are stuck in place on the paper backing, the next step is to check for any loose ones, then cover with a piece of heavy cardboard or light plywood. Prepare mortar bed slightly deeper than the thickest piece in the mosaic. Turn mosaic over, and slide it from the cardboard as you lower the underside of it into the mortar. Level the paper-covered top surface by pressing it down gently with a flat board. When mortar is set, peel away the paper. Dampen paper if paste was used.

So much for methods in general. Some specific details will be taken up as they are concerned with special materials. The following pages are given over to descriptions and working details of actual surfacing materials we have found to be practical and interesting. Some of them are traditional materials. Others are not so commonly used. We set them forth in the categories of glass, clay, wood, linoleum, stone and seeds. Take your choice—but plan to start a mosaic right away!

To make a level surface when you set the tesserae directly on a rigid base, use materials of all the same thickness.

Pebbles set directly in fresh mortar can be tapped gently with a hammer to set them down and make them conform to a level.

Make a level surface of irregular thickness of material by pasting them to paper face down. Then turn mosaic and lower the underside of it into a bed of fresh mortar.

When the mortar is dry under the mosaic which has been lowered into it, peel off the paper tesserae were set on originally.

glass tiles

The colorful pressed glass squares from Italy or Mexico are a first choice of mosaic materials for many. You may find them in other shapes and sizes but most of these tiles are ¾″ square and about ¼″ thick although thickness varies from brand to brand. They are shipped pasted face-down on foot-square sheets of brown paper, 225 of them to a sheet. You buy them by the sheet, half sheet, sometimes by the "line" (a strip across the square of 16 tiles) or even singly. The light neutral colors cost the least, usually a penny apiece if bought singly; the strong, bright colors and metallics cost the most. Since there are now so many brands and suppliers of this material and price varies according to source and quantities purchased, it will pay to shop. The Mexican tiles cost less than the Italian but come in fewer colors.

Either can be used for outdoor projects as they are vitreous and non-absorbent. They make serviceable, handsome counter and table tops as well as smaller accessories.

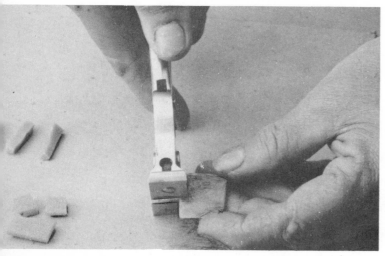

Glass tiles are laid in either the direct or indirect methods on rigid backing with white glue or tile setting mastic.

To prepare tile for use, first soak the sheets of pasted-down tiles in warm water and peel away backing paper. Rinse and dry. Store colors separately in glass jars.

If you want glass tile surface to be flat and smooth for table or counter, be sure that tiles you use are all the same brand.

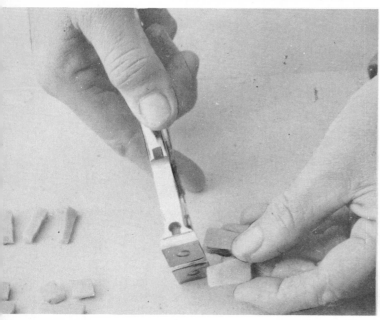

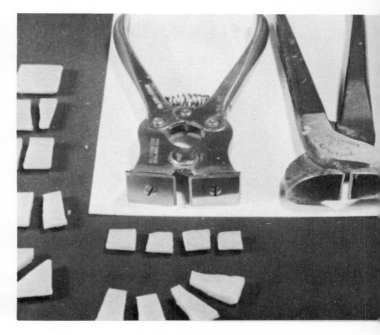

The glass is really fractured, rather than cut. Hold tile between thumb and fingers of one hand, put cutter blades so they just nip tile edge and press. Tile breaks across at angle of nipper jaws. Hold tile face side up, cut to make two half tiles. Then, to make quarter cuts, nip halves in two again. Cut across corners to make half-triangles, in half again to make quarter triangles.

Most projects will call for breaking or cutting at least some of the tiles. Nippers and cutters come in several styles—see a choice where you buy tile. Any of them will do a good job once you acquire the "knack" of cutting. Thick tiles cut more accurately than thin; some colors cut better than others. Glass varies, so if much cutting is to be done do buy and cut a test batch as a starting step.

smalti

This Byzantine glass from Italy is the important traditional mosaic material. Smalti, the trade name for this glass, comes in rectangles about ⅜″ x ½″, 5/16″ thick. Dimensions, edges and thickness are all irregular. Smalti is sold by the pound; priced according to color, in hundreds of color shades. Bright reds may cost as much as $6 a pound and it takes about two pounds to cover one square foot. It is, therefore, an expensive material as mosaic materials go and we usually reserve it for small bright accessories and sculptured projects.

Smalti can be combined in interesting effects with scrap glass, squares cut from stained glass sheets and, rather surprisingly, with rectangles of comparable size cut from unglazed ceramic tiles.

Smalti is ready to use just as it comes. If you need smaller pieces you can cut them with a cold chisel and hammer. Just put the chisel blade across rectangle where you want to cut and strike end of it with the hammer. Best do the cutting inside a box as pieces fly.

Do protect the eyes with glasses or goggles however you cut smalti—and you may prefer regular tile nippers for this. To cut with nippers, choose the thinner pieces and cut across the face of the rectangle instead of at an edge as you do with the glass tiles. To nip in half or cut off a corner, put it in jaws of cutter and hold cutter over palm of hand to catch the pieces when you cut. You can also cut smalti on a hardie as shown on page 37.

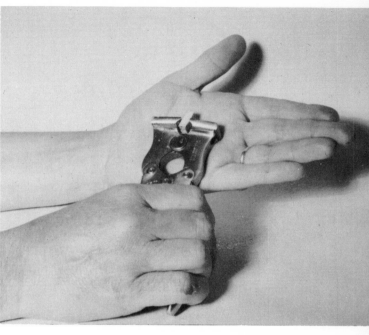

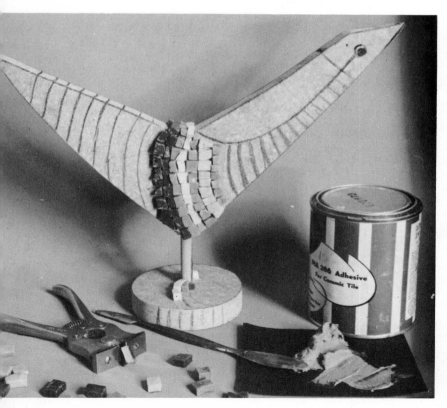

Smalti can be set directly on any rigid surface with white glue or tile setting mastic. Use the mastic if setting surface is vertical. The direct method makes a very rough texture with depth and richness. Grouting is inadvisable when smalti is set this way. Smalti can be set directly with a smoother, although not absolutely level, effect by setting it in a bed of mortar made with fine sand and Portland cement. Use two parts sand, one part cement and add one teaspoon cement bonding adhesive to each pint of mixing water. Mix a small amount of mortar at a time, just enough to set a half pound or so of smalti at a time.

The flattest, easiest to clean smalti mosaic surface is made by the indirect method. Pieces are pasted to design areas drawn in reverse on brown paper; sections turned over and lowered into prepared mortar.

stained glass

Brilliant translucent mosaics can be made with colored glass pieces set on a base of clear glass or plastic. You can use pieces of colored glass on opaque backing but it will lose both color and brilliance unless the backing material is light-colored or metallic. Metallic spray paints can be used to spray either the backing material or the back of the glass.

Stained glass comes in a wonderful range of color and some of it has pebbled and textured finishes. If you are near a commercial studio that makes stained glass windows you may be able to buy scraps of this glass by the pound. If not, experiment by color-spraying the back of ordinary window glass. Pieces of broken glass plates, even broken mirror glass, can be used to advantage.

Use colored glass in layers or in combination with opaque materials, letting light through some areas, but not others. There is lots of room for experiment in the use of glass in mosaics.

Cutting glass into small squares and rectangles for mosaic making is easy if you have a sharp glass cutter. Buy the kind with the round wheel on one end of the handle, the round iron ball on the other.

To cut, lay glass flat and score it in free-hand lines about ½″ apart. Draw glass cutter along evenly, using just enough pressure to hear the cutter "bite" the glass surface. Score across the first set of lines to make rectangles. Turn glass over and tap it with the ball end of the tool along the scored lines. It will break along the lines.

You needn't get cut handling and cutting glass if you take care. Never pick up glass pieces by the edge. Never brush glass crumbs with the fingers—use a brush.

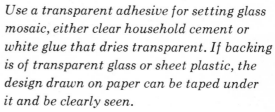

Use a transparent adhesive for setting glass mosaic, either clear household cement or white glue that dries transparent. If backing is of transparent glass or sheet plastic, the design drawn on paper can be taped under it and be clearly seen.

Sheet glass mosaic can be left ungrouted or grouted with regular ceramic tile grout. The cracks can be filled and the surface leveled by pouring a coat of liquid plastic over it. Buy the liquid plastic syrup sold for fibre-glassing boat decks. Cover edges, frames, etc., with drafting tape to prevent leaks and stains before pouring plastic. Protect working surface with newspapers.

bottle glass

Colored bottles can be broken to make mosaic material. This material can be said to be both plentiful and cheap. Impervious to weather or wear, it can be used indoors or out. Handling the sharp pieces can be hazardous, however, and certain treatments are advisable to make it safer to handle.

One way to improve raw broken glass is to melt the edges down in a ceramic kiln. Another is to tumble it in a can with sharp sand and water until edges are rounded and surfaces sanded like the glass you find on the beach. An easy-to-make tumbler is diagrammed at the bottom of this page.

These pieces of melted glass look like oversize drops of water. They are particularly elegant when set on glass or plastic with a transparent adhesive to make translucent panels.

The best way to break a bottle with safety is to put it inside several brown paper bags. Hold bags together at their tops, strike covered bottle with hammer. Look in and see if pieces are small enough—if not, close bags and pound some more. Tear bags down one side and pick out bottle pieces you want.

Put a layer of powdered "kiln wash" on shelf and bottom of kiln when you melt glass laid directly on them. Keep pieces in from the edge. Heat kiln to almost a white heat— you can peek and observe stage of melting— or use .07 cones. Let kiln cool with door closed.

You can make glass "pancakes" for breaking or cutting in pieces by putting smaller scraps in flower pot saucers that have been coated inside with kiln wash to keep the glass from sticking and firing to melting point of the glass. Don't open kiln door while it is hot or the flower pot saucers may crack.

ceramic tile

There are many kinds of clay tiles; and pieces cut or broken from any of them make good mosaic material. Some ceramic tiles have a top coating of a hard, shiny glaze, some have a smooth, dull glaze, others have no surface finish at all. The colors of these tile are the colors of the clays they are made of and they will be the same color all the way through. This is the type often used in floors and it makes a good choice for mosaic floors and paving because there is no glaze to scratch or wear. Glazed tile is tough enough, with the exception of some of the metallics, for use as table and counter top mosaic.

You can buy mosaic tile in squares ¾″, sometimes larger or smaller. Ceramic tile is also sold at tile setting stores who do kitchen and bath tiling—these stores may also have scrap material for sale by the pound. You can sometimes find scrap tile or used tile in land fills or on dumps.

Most ceramic tile can be cut with nippers. We show it here being cut on a hardie as it is a good tool to know about, handy for cutting smalti and marble as well as tile. Hardie is a wide chisel blade with a shaft meant to set in a hole in a blacksmith's anvil. Buy a hardie at a "heavy hardware" store or junk yard and make base by setting it in a can of concrete or have sheet iron square welded on shaft bottom.

To cut a strip of tile on the hardie, place it across blade where you want it to break and strike it with the blade of a shoemaker's hammer or the square end of a sheet metal hammer. A short, quick stroke makes the best break, may take a little practice.

Set glazed ceramic tile directly on a rigid base or in a soft mortar bed. If you want to use them in indirect method, paste to paper background right-side up. Then paste heavy cloth or paper over right side and turn upside down and gently sponge and peel off bottom paper. Then lower bottoms of tile pieces thus exposed into prepared mortar bed.

broken pottery

Fragments of glazed pottery make a mosaic material that is color-ful, inexpensive and easily obtained. Household accidents may provide some of it. You can acquire choice colors by buying chipped or cracked plates and saucers for a few cents apiece at rummage sales and charity-managed stores. Or you may know a potter, either professional or hobbyist, who will sell or give away imperfect pieces. Handmade ceramic glazes can be very special in both color and texture and they will combine well with many other mosaic materials.

Use pottery pieces in mosaics to be placed indoors or out, as long as they will not be subjected to severe freezing or hard abrasion. Pottery shapes that break to make fragments with concave and convex curves add glitter and interest to mosaic panels. The curves flatten as pieces are made smaller and these can be used for flat surfaced mosaics.

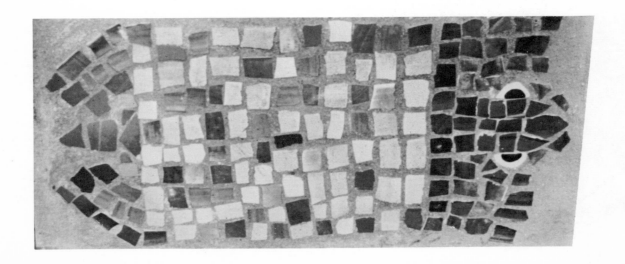

Use rigid board, either plywood or one of the pressed wood hardboards, for backing of broken pottery mosaic. Glue the pieces in place on the backing with white glue or ceramic-tile setting paste. Larger pottery pieces, particularly those with convex or concave surfaces, make good material for setting in mortar, either cement or spackle.

Ceramists can make good use of left-overs from glaze batches by firing them on thin clay slabs and breaking these for mosaic.

Unglazed clay pottery, such as the common terra-cotta flower pot, also makes useful mosaic material. The soft colors and the matte surfaces of the unglazed clay combine well with pebbles and unpolished marble cubes and chips.

To make mosaic material from broken dishes, put the larger pieces inside an old magazine and pound the closed magazine with a hammer. This method will keep pottery shards from scattering.

Most pottery materials can be cut with tile cutting nippers. Shape the hammer-smashed shards into small rectangles and triangles by nipping a larger piece in half, then in half again until desired size is reached.

linoleum

Asphalt, rubber or vinyl linoleum makes a mosaic material with several special advantages. It is easy to cut and clean to handle; is inexpensive and readily available. These features make it a good choice for children's projects.

Linoleum is especially practical for mosaic table tops, sink boards and counter tops; serving trays and splash panels behind wash basins, sinks and ranges. It makes a quiet, resilient surface that wears well and wipes clean. Because it is lightweight, use it for portable panels.

You'll find linoleum in many colors—in marbleized and spatter combinations as well as plain. Build your color palette by buying separate 9″ square floor tiles or collecting scraps. To find sources of supply, look up Floor Materials in the Yellow Section of your phone book.

Cut linoleum with scissors or tin snips. Warm material very slightly if it tends to crack or split as you cut it. Any size or shape of tesserae is readily cut but small irregular rectangles ½″ to 1½″ work out well in most designs.

Use ⅜″ to ½″ plywood or hardboard for backing. Designs are drawn or traced directly on the board. Stick tesserae in place with white glue or ceramic adhesive paste—use the latter if waterproofing is important.

If an absolute level surface is desired use linoleum of the same thickness throughout.

When mosaic pieces are all in place run fingers over surface to locate any loose ones. When all are firmly in place mosaic can be grouted. Use ceramic tile grout mixed with cold water to make a thick, creamy paste. A rubber spatula is a good tool for pressing grout in cracks. Let grout set a few minutes then wipe surface clean. Use soft cloths, dry or dampened very slightly. Grout dries quickly so it is best to grout an area of not more than two or three square feet at a time.

When grout is thoroughly dry moisten a soft cloth with silicone waterproofing and polish the entire mosaic surface. Further polishing can be done with paste wax applied in light, well-rubbed coats.

pebbles and stones

Small stones and pebbles are classic mosaic material. They make beautiful and enduring mosaic patterns to be used either indoors or out—impervious to weather or wear—and requiring no special upkeep.

Collecting pebbles for mosaic making is fun the whole family can enjoy. A young mother we know says, "Even the baby brings me pebbles!" Pebbles and stones are to be had just for the finding, or you can buy them. They are sold in bulk at concrete and aggregate yards. Florists and importers of novelties have them sorted and boxed for flower arrangers. Special stones for accents or highlight are sold at lapidary shops. Garden supply shops often sell pebbles or stone chips by the pound.

Before you begin, sort pebbles for color and size. Wash to remove earth or salt. Dry and store in rust-proof containers to avoid stains.

Pebbles can be set on rigid backing panels and on existing vertical surfaces with tile-setting paste and grouted with ceramic tile grout. This is a good method where light weight is important and a level surface is not.

Pebbles are usually set in a base of wet mortar. Buy a bag of dry ready-mixed mortar, adding water as directed, or make your own by mixing three parts sand and one part Portland cement, adding sufficient water to make a thick, creamy paste. In modern practice, a cement bonding adhesive (buy it where dry mortar mix is sold) is added to the water. Use about three tablespoons adhesive to a gallon of water.

Lay pebbles in wet concrete and sink firmly. Use a flat board on level surfaces. Taps with a light hammer will help on curved surfaces such as that on the birdbath shown here.

Mrs. Frederick Keast, at work on the bird bath shown here, likes to combine pebbles with lapidary-cut slabs of ornamental stone.

Cement colors in the form of dry powders are mixed with dry mortar. Test mortar color by adding water to a small amount of colored mix and letting it dry. Dark color mortars with dark colored pebbles and light colored mortars with light pebbles gives greater unity to pebble patterns.

Cover finished sections of pebble mosaic with damp cloths and let them dry slowly and undisturbed. If pebbles should come loose, replace with a coat of undiluted concrete adhesive.

marble

The polished and unpolished marbles combine with good effect to make handsome mosaics. The many colors of this stone are subdued and subtle; strongest in the polished pieces. Marble for mosaics is usually begged, sometimes bought, from the scrap piles of trimmings and waste materials from the marble works. You might find some on the city dump or in land fills. When sorting scrap stone, choose thin slabs that can be broken with a hammer to random shapes and strips that can be cut across with hammer and chisel to make cubes.

To make a level surface with marble cubes, set them directly in concrete mortar or in mortar by the reverse method. To do this, first reverse design to be used by turning it over and tracing on heavy brown paper. Then use flour paste or rubber cement to stick marble pieces face down on the design. When all pieces are pasted down, check carefully for loose ones, as entire mosaic must be turned over to lower it into mortar bed.

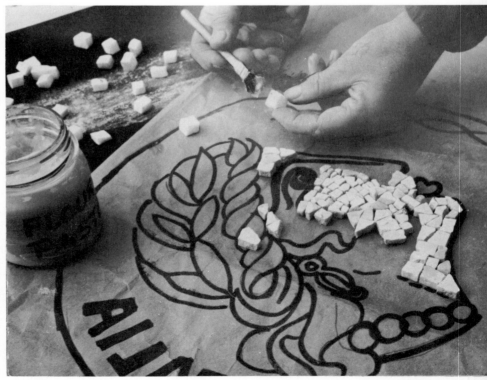

To break thin, polished sheets of scrap marble in random pieces, cover with cardboard and strike with hammer blows. Do protect eyes by wearing glasses, goggles or plastic face mask.

To cut cubes from rectangular strips of scrap marble, use a sharpened cold chisel or sculptor's chisel and hammer. The light-colored marbles can be further shaped with tile-cutting nippers. Edges of marble cubes can be smoothed by rubbing them over coarse emery paper.

Make mortar for setting marble by mixing two parts fine sand with one part Portland cement and adding water to make a thick creamy paste. Mortar bed must be deep enough to accommodate the thickest marble pieces if surface is to be level. Press mosaic, paper side up, firmly into mortar. Level by tapping over surface with flat board or gently rolling it with a wooden rolling pin. When mortar has set hard enough to hold pieces, carefully peel back paper—again checking for loose bits. Cover finished mosaic with damp cloth to cure for several days, then scour and clean surface.

wood

Scrap or waste wood found on the wood pile, in the scrap bin at the lumber yard or as driftwood makes unusual mosaic material. Even common woods when newly cut are quite colorful; you'll find tans, cream colors and reddish browns. Old wood is grey, brown or almost black. Beaches, tide flats and river banks yield old boards bleached and silvered by the elements—timbers textured by decay or the busywork of insects. In the eyes of some people this wood has a special character and much beauty. If you like it, do try a wood mosaic.

Wood mosaic panels make good exterior decoration. They will add interest to fences, gates, on entrance walls or as space dividers in outdoor "rooms."

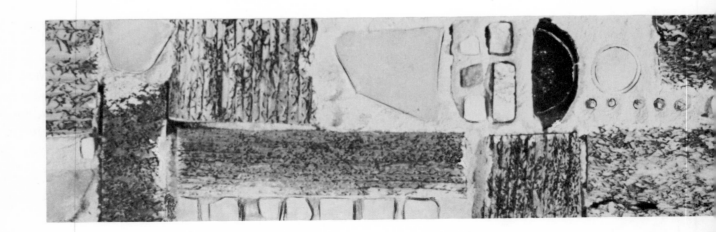

Use any good wood glue to set wood mosaic pieces on a backing board. They can also be set in concrete mortar which has had concrete bonding adhesive added to it. See directions for setting pebbles in mortar.

Give finished mosaic a coat or two of a wood finish designed to hold wood color. Ask your lumber or building supply dealer about these.

Driftwood is full of sand—salvaged wood is bound to conceal a few nails. Both will ruin a good saw so use an old one even if it slows the work of cutting wood for mosaic.

Scrub weathered wood surfaces with a stiff wire brush to remove soft fibres and bring out interesting grain. Wood stains or shoe polish will color and darken it— household laundry bleaches lighten it.

Sometimes scraps of wood suggest a form. This was the case with our Perching Bird. Children love these "just for fun" mosaics. Bird sections were simply nailed to a backing board, the background spaces filled with concrete mortar.

seeds

Individual seeds, chosen for color and shape and set side by side in mosaic arrangement, add up to create textures and patterns of surprising beauty. The finished effect is that of tapestry.

Materials for seed mosaics are everywhere. Cost is a minor point. Weeds, trees and shrubs near you are sure to provide pods and seeds you can use. Look for them on your kitchen shelves, in grocery and feed stores. Consider only a few possibilities—split peas, beans, lentils and barley—and you'll think of many more.

Seed mosaics are best used as framed pictures or wall panels. If used for a utilitarian surface, such as that of a coffee table, the mosaic must be under glass or clear plastic.

Creating a seed mosaic can be fascinating or frustrating. The results make the work most worthwhile if you like to handle small units and can use tweezers readily.

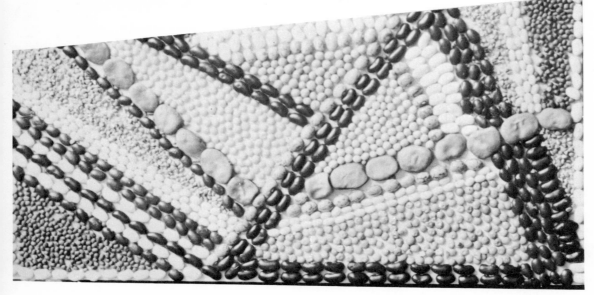

Prepare seeds for mosaic use by heating
them in a 350 degree oven for 15 minutes
to discourage germination and weevils.
Heat may change the color of some seeds.

Keep kinds of seeds in separate containers so
you needn't sort and pick for color and kind.

The most effective designs for seed mosaics are
those with simple shapes and strong outlines.
Designs can be drawn or traced on the mosaic
backing.

The backing for a seed mosaic should be
rigid enough to keep it from bending or
buckling. Use pressed pulp or plywood.

The best adhesive for seeds is white glue.
Spread it with a brush over a small area
at a time, then set seeds. Large seeds are
set one at a time with tweezers or pushed
in place with a small pointed stick. They
look best when set uniformly, such as all
pointing one way or with eyes right or left.
Small seeds can be sprinkled over glue-spread
areas in pinches or by the handful, and this
speeds the covering of background spaces.

Check the finished mosaic for any loose seeds.
Use glue in drops from spout of plastic dis-
penser when replacing seeds. When all seeds
are firmly in place and glue is thoroughly dry
give mosaic several coats of clear plastic spray.

This panel planned for a garden will have a design of fruit and vines. Material will be glazed ceramic tile.

color and
design for mosaics

In mosaic making you build design, pattern and texture by placing small bits of mosaic material side by side. You choose, and use, colors available to you in the material you select for your mosaic. There is pleasure in the very simplicity of these things. There are a few things to consider in choosing designs and colors for a successful mosaic, however, and these factors are the subject of this chapter.

In designing a mosaic and selecting the colors for it, begin by considering your chosen material. It will not matter which you decide on for a first mosaic but do plan to use just one kind. Advanced mosaicists mix materials with good results but it isn't easy—although it may look to be. One difficulty in mixing materials lies in the fact that it usually means mixing shapes since each material either comes in certain shapes or naturally falls into them when cut or broken. If used unskillfully, the shapes of the pieces dominate the design to destroy the unity of material and design that makes a good mosaic.

Good design in any medium depends on unity, harmony and

simplicity—and simplicity makes it easier to get harmony and unity. This is why most mosaics, traditionally and in modern practice, use tesserae of the same kind and of about the same shape and size throughout.

The best designs for mosaic are those with mass and broad lines. Fine lines and small, complex areas are obviously unsuitable. This is why it will be better to do your designing with a big brush or with paper and scissors. A pencil, familiar to most of us as a writing tool only, leads to dinky detail that doesn't translate into mosaic.

If you are using one of the "starter" designs given in this book, enlarge it by dividing your paper into squares. Make as many squares on your paper as there are behind the printed design— count them down one side and across one end. Then copy the lines that show in each square of the printed design.

The next step is to consider your design in terms of your material. Spread a few of your tesserae out on the paper within the areas you'll be covering with them. You may find the areas too small for the size of the mosaic pieces—that they are going to make the design hard to "see." In this case change the design. This often means simplifying it by using fewer areas and this can be an improvement.

The size of your design has a bearing on how effective it will be when done in a given material. A design two feet square that is just right for split peas and beans may be all wrong for smalti, for instance. So even though you are using a design that has been done in mosaic before it is a good idea to "try it for size" before going ahead with the actual materials.

Make your own designs to make the most of the mosaic making experience. If a pencil inhibits designing ability, use paper and scissors. Try cutting shapes from colored construction paper. Lay these in various arrangements over a sheet of paper the size your finished mosaic is to be — this helps determine color choices, too.

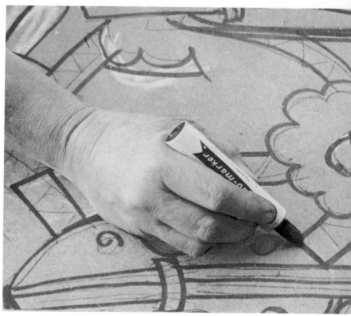

When your design has been chalked or traced on the mosaic base, go over it to strengthen the lines you want to keep. Use heavy pencil, wax crayon or a felt marking pen.

Mosaic designs can be somewhat sketchy indications of lines and area rather than positive, definite outlines because the actual materials may dictate some changes.

Color, perhaps the most important and appealing part of a mosaic is decided on next. Look over the color range of your material. Some come in many colors, some in few. It isn't the number of colors you use, but how you use them that counts. If you must choose from an unlimited range, here are a few suggestions.

First, the smaller the mosaic, the fewer colors will be needed. A tray, for instance, may work out handsomely in three colors, fail if more than five are used. This is only a suggestion, not a rule.

Here are more color suggestions. Choose and use colors of different kinds. Some are bright, like red, some dark, like navy blue. Use these in small amounts for accents. Every color scheme benefits by at least one accent color. Other colors are dull, such as grey, or light, as pastel pink. Most color schemes will use several dull or light colors. The design on a tray might use a dull or neutral color for the background, one or two light colors for the design motif and a vivid or strong dark color for accenting a small but important part of the motif. A larger mosaic can use a larger number of colors but it would still require the same balance between bright and dark, dull and light colors.

It is easy to visualize colors as they will be in a small design. If your design is large, help your imagination by getting out your design and putting a few of the colored tesserae down in the areas they are to fill. This is usually more effective than trying to color the areas with crayons or paint. You can move your pieces around to try several arrangements. When you get one that pleases, make color notes on your drawing or paste down a sample piece.

If your project calls for sticking mosaic pieces directly to a rigid backing—and this is about the best way for a beginner to work—

When more than one material suggests itself
for a project, it is best to lay some of the
pieces of material in place as they will be
used and look at them. We first thought
pebbles would be right for this garden
sculpture but later decided against them.

We eventually chose shards of colored glass—
mostly blues—for the garden goose. Glass
was melted in the kiln to round edges and
then set on the lightweight concrete form
with concrete bonding adhesive and pure
Portland cement mixed to a thick paste.

your next step will be to transfer your design to the backing. A small, simple design can be sketched free-hand right on the wood. Start with chalked lines, then darken lines you want to keep with crayon, heavy pencil or a felt marker. Use carbon paper for tracing more intricate designs or rub a soft pencil over the back of your drawing and go over lines again.

Now you are ready to start setting your mosaic pieces. Fill in the main areas first. If you want the outlines of certain areas to be especially well defined, start by placing your pieces along these lines. As you fill an area, note whether the pieces tend to flow along smoothly. Experiment to find the best way to fit your pieces of material into your areas.

Stand back once in awhile as the work progresses and look at it from a distance. Does the design "carry"? The effect of a mosaic is sometimes easier to judge if viewed at an angle—this tends to make the cracks and unfinished areas less confusing to the eye. Colors of adjoining shapes should contrast enough to make the design clear and interesting and placement of the pieces shouldn't form awkward shapes. It is possible to pry up pieces and change them after they are glued—but it is obviously much easier to make changes before gluing.

When all the pieces are in place and the glue is dry you can decide on grouting. Trays, table tops and such surfaces must be grouted for sanitary reasons. Pictures or panels can be grouted or not, as you please. White or light grout sometimes seems to rob mosaic of its color and character. Matching the grout to the background or predominating color usually gives a better effect.

The dry powder colors are mixed with dry grout—shake grout

Remember that the spaces between the tesserae are part of the design, too, and that these can be used to suggest lines and details. Incidentally, cracks may be wide or narrow but they look best when fairly uniform in width.

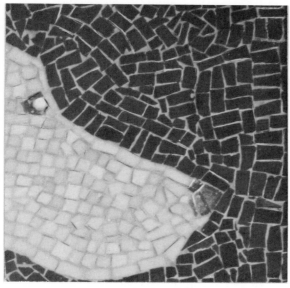

Large areas and background spaces will be most effective if they are made up of pieces laid to some simple plan. They may make an irregular pattern that repeats over the area. This is a close-up of such a pattern taken from the portrait of dog done by Mrs. Bean on page 15.

Background lines may also follow the contours made by the outlines of the design motifs, or be laid in gently wavy or curved lines, either vertical or horizontal.

It is always a good plan to try and work out designs in terms of the material shapes. If pieces do not follow lines and fill areas easily, change the design a little as you go along. Some pieces will be ground or cut to special shapes, but greater unity results when special shaping is kept to a minimum.

and color together in a jar for good distribution—and the water added to the colored grout. Another way is to add poster paint or water color to the wet grout mix. Remember that grout colors dry lighter than they look when they are wet. If you are particular about obtaining a special shade, mix a dab or so and let it dry before mixing the whole batch.

When the colored grout is dry, rub the whole surface with a silicone solution to waterproof the grout and hold the color—this is especially important if water colors have been used.

Concrete mortars and mixes can be colored, too. Natural grey concrete makes duller, "dusty" colors—more brilliant colors may be had with white concrete. Buy cement colors that resist the lime in cement. You can get them at building supply stores and lumber yards where concrete and mortar are sold. Mix dry color with dry ingredients. Mix enough for the job as these colors are hard to match.

Colored mortar looks well with pebbles, marble or glass. It is interesting to color separate sections to match or contrast with the mosaic pieces used in the section.

It would take much more than one chapter, indeed more than one book, to say everything that might be said about color and design for mosaic! We hope you can make a start with the suggestions given here. You may not want to follow all of them. It may seem easier to just go ahead and make a small mosaic and see how it turns out. If you do this, and the results aren't all you hoped for, re-read the chapter again. You may find the suggestions even more helpful on a second mosaic.

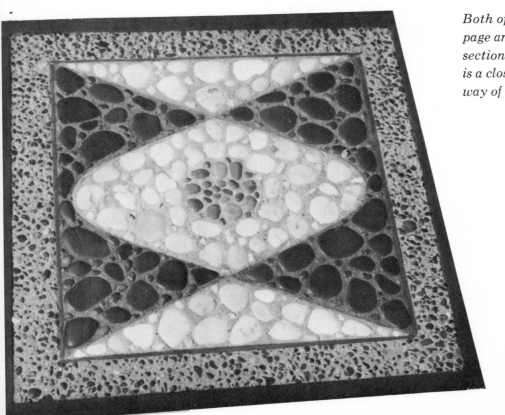

Pebble patterns are stronger, shapes more definite when the setting mortar is mixed with dry color. Use dark mortar with dark stones; light colored mixes with white and grey stones.

If colored mortar sections are not confined within wood or metal dividing strips, cut excess mortar away after it stiffens but before it actually sets. Brush set concrete with bonding adhesive before adding a fresh concrete section.

Both of the handsome pebble mosaics on this page are the work of Edith Hamlin. The section of pebble paving with marine motifs is a close-up detail of the paving in the entry way of her San Francisco studio.

mosaic projects
for the house

All the mosaic projects we discuss in this book are domestic—things meant to live with in home surroundings. The panel on the opposite page, for instance, is mounted behind the kitchen stove in our adobe house. We have used the Aztec design motifs elsewhere in the room so this mosaic is at home with us—and we like to think that it makes our home even more distinctively ours.

Mosaics made by you, for your home, should fill your exact wants and needs. You can have them in the colors of your choice with the kind of design motifs you like. The projects you choose to make will depend on how you live and the things you like to live with. In the following paragraphs of suggestions for things that might be decorated with mosaic there are bound to be some you will enjoy making and owning.

If you find mosaic making as pleasurable as we hope you will, you'll make mosaics as gifts, too. Small household accessories are quickly made and they will be appreciated as "hostess" thank-you gifts or a present for a whole family at Christmas.

Mosaic surfaces are wonderfully care-free for kitchens and bathrooms. Use them for counter and table tops, for splash panels behind sinks and washbasins. Smaller mosaics can adorn trays, breadboards, line fruit bowls and ashtrays, cover canisters and waste baskets. A panel to mount behind a row of copper pots or good looking stainless steel utensils is decorative in the kitchen.

Not all our projects are strictly functional—some are pictures and design panels meant for entry halls, children's rooms, living and dining rooms and play or work rooms. In the dining room there is need for hot pads—make a nice big one for a platter—for candlesticks and cigarette boxes. Small panels behind switch plates and as push panels on swinging doors are easy to wipe clean.

Special tables in the living room—coffee, cocktail or game tables —make interesting projects. Cabinet doors and panels on some pieces of furniture offer possibilities. Lamp bases, book ends and clock faces are other practical projects.

Small sculptural forms of birds and animals are unusual bases for mosaic. These bases can be very simple, little more than a silhouette of the bird or animal sawed from plywood. Mosaic can be applied to one side only and the piece used as a plaque or it can have mosaic on both sides and edges and be free standing.

As with any lively interest, idea follows on the heels of idea, and you'll not lack inspiration for things to decorate with mosaic. In the following pages are some of the things we did in mosaic. Most of them were done especially for this book.

bread board

First cut base board about 7″ wide and 13″ long. Ash, birch or maple are good hardwoods for this project. Smooth one surface for the bread slicing side. Cut a piece of solid color linoleum to cover the other side. Trace cat motif in place on this background and cut it out to leave a cat-shape opening. Glue to the baseboard, then fill in opening with linoleum tesserae. When glue is dry, fill cracks with ceramic tile grout and wipe mosaic clean. Sand edges so linoleum is flush with the wood.

tv tray

This is a tray that our neighbor, Mrs. Victor Naglik, made for her youngest son. Note how the shape of the linoleum pieces form the design. Black and yellow strips alternate to make the mane; features and toenails are black. Any round tray—this one is about 14″ in diameter—of metal or wood will make a base for this project. Sandpaper the center of shiny or slick new trays—spray paint or enamel around the rim before decorating an old tray.

jack of spades

This design, intended for a rumpus room, was borrowed from one on an ancient playing card. Vinyl plastic linoleum tile provides the warm bright colors used in it. The figure is done in shades of red, orange, yellow and yellow green with accents of black. Face and hands are white; background is done in shades of blue. This panel is 23½″ x 15″. The linoleum pieces were glued directly to the framed plywood panel with the front edge of the frame flush with the surface of the mosaic. Panel is not grouted.

fruit plate

The base for this project is a 10½″ disk of hardwood with a large cork mounted at the center to hold the set of fruit knives. We turned the wood circle on the wood lathe, lowering the area to be set with the Venetian tile strips. Any round tray could be used, however. The colors on our fruit plate tinge from pale cream to dark brown. Occasional strips of vermillion make bright accents.

snack board

The size and shape of this board—21″ long and 6½″ at the widest part—make it just right for a long loaf of French bread. Small porcelain tiles were used to make the 5½″ circular insert. This area was carved to lower it so tiles, when set in, are flush with the surrounding wood. The snack board has a footing board cut 1″ smaller at sides and the knife blades slip into slots left between cutting and bottom boards.

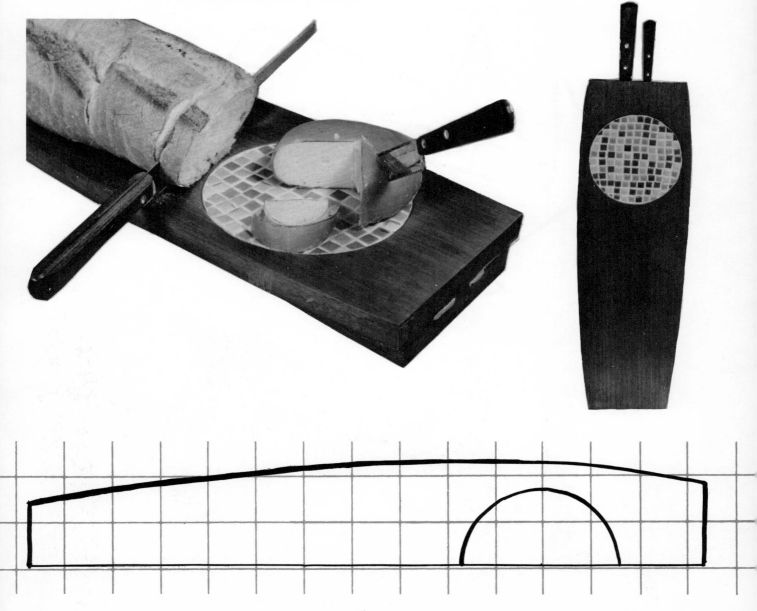

serving tray

The translucent mosaic that makes the surface of this tray was made by sticking tesserae cut from scrap stained glass onto sheet plastic, then covering it with a thin coat of plastic resin. The resin binds it to the sheet plastic and fills the cracks between the colored glass pieces at the same time. Any glass surfaced tray can be used— we replaced the glass in an old tray with ⅛″ sheet plastic as being more practical than glass.

harlequin

The figure in this panel is made with pieces of broken plates. The bright-colored glazes and the angular shapes natural to the material make it particularly suited to the design. The diamond pattern of the pants offers such a fine opportunity to use lots of colors—and we made the most of it, using blues, green-blues, dusty pinks, browns, yellows and gold. The pottery pieces were glued directly to the plywood panel. The mosaic is not grouted but the background space is filled with a troweled-on layer of patching plaster compound mixed with vermiculite. You can buy vermiculite in small quantities in florists and at garden stores.

quail

Seeds seem an appropriate material for this mosaic, and the dining room a suitable place to hang the finished picture. The over-all tone of this panel is tawny because seeds used to make it are yellow split peas, tan whole peas, brown rice and coffee beans in both dark and light roast—the dark roast is almost black. White beans form accent areas. Larger seeds were glued to the plywood backing one at a time—the brown rice background sprinkled on and pressed into a layer of fresh glue. Picture is 21″ by 15½″.

owl and pussy cat

This pair, well-known in most nurseries, are shown here as they make their nocturnal voyage in the beautiful pea-green boat. Do you remember how the owl looked up to the stars and sang to a small guitar? In this mosaic of Venetian glass tile, moon and stars are pale yellow in a sky of dull grey-blues. The sea is in shades of blue and blue-green—fish are salmon and the beautiful Pussy is in shades of white with blue eyes. This picture, made for a child's room is 27″ x 19″.

plant table

Sections of polished redwood in natural color contrast with pebbled sections in this table. Black, grey and dark red pebbles were set directly on the plywood backing with ceramic tile setting mastic, then grouted with ceramic tile grout. Redwood sections were glued in place first. Pebbles could be set in concrete mortar if wood surfaces were well protected while this was being done. Give table top a finish of a waterproofing silica solution.

towel holders

These obliging fish will make a bright touch in kitchen or bathroom. The backing form is first cut from plywood. Black harness ring is fastened to the plywood with a loop of soft aluminum. Cut metal strip, drill both ends, run through the ring and fasten ends to back of the plywood form with a flat head screw. Mosaic is made with Italian smalti set in spackle.

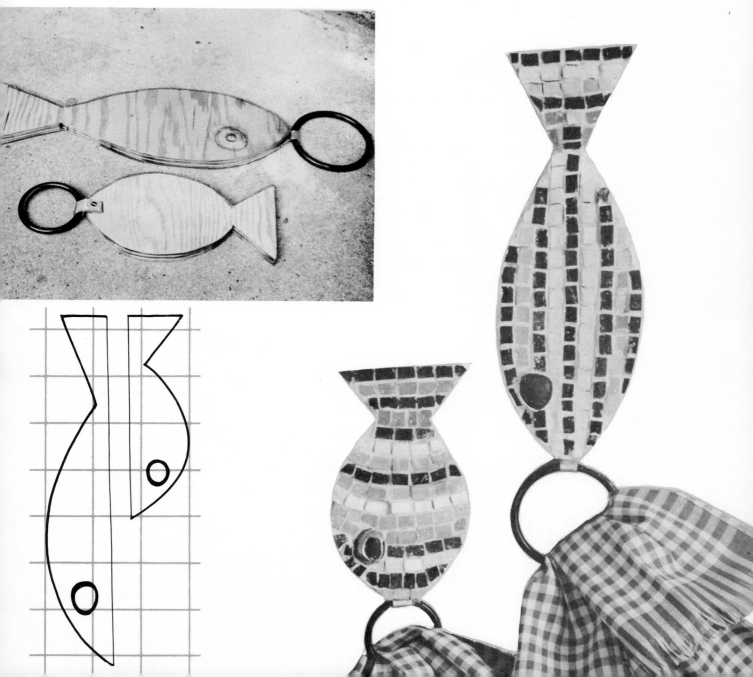

hi-fi cabinet

This cabinet, bought unfinished, becomes a distinguished piece of furniture with the addition of a mosaic panel done in vinyl linoleum. There are many pieces of unfinished furniture that would be fun to decorate in this way—storage cabinets with sliding doors, portable bars, desks and dressing tables, even drawer fronts in chests could be surfaced with mosaic.

occasional table

This little table was in sad shape when we rescued it from a junk yard. The pierced brass rim was bent, the original marble inset on the top mostly gone. It suggested a marble mosaic in this formal design taken from an old Roman coin. Hand-cut marble rectangles were set by the reverse method to make the new marble surface. See pages 44 and 45 for details of reverse method of mosaic setting.

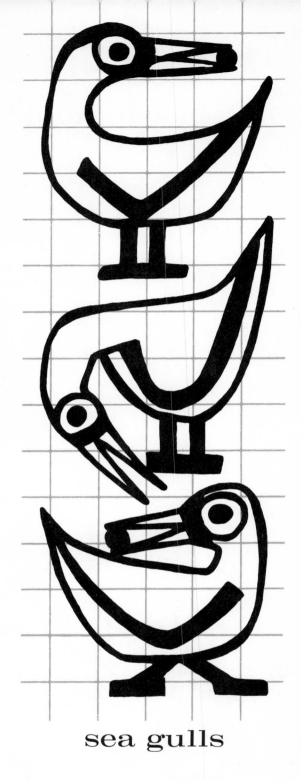

sea gulls

The mahogany-veneered surface of the plywood backing of this panel also serves as the background of the mosaic. The mosaic surface was made level with the wood by carving the veneer top layer of the plywood away where linoleum mosaic motifs were to be set. Use carpenter's or wood carving chisels—cut straight down along outline of motif, then cut layer of wood within away. Mosaic areas are grouted.

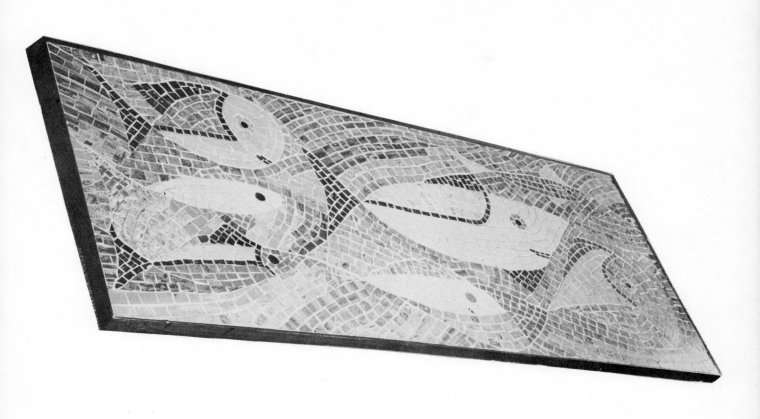

coffee table

This is a large table—over 5' long—but the work of laying the
mosaic went quickly because the small linoleum rectangles that
make it were cut in wholesale lots, then set in flowing rows directly
on the plywood backing. Large objects like this are good ones for
mosaic making teams.

A lightweight concrete form, surfaced with black pebbles and concrete mortar makes an amusing garden sculpture.

mosaic projects
for the garden

Mosaic projects will add both color and personality to the patio and garden. Mosaic textures, particularly the stronger ones of wood, bottle glass and stones are beautiful with plant materials and exterior building materials. Rough wood siding, fencing, brick or adobe walls, concrete paving—these are all good companions for mosaic.

As you'll know by now, outdoor mosaic is thoroughly practical if you choose and use the weatherproof tesserae of glass, wood or pebbles on marine plywood or metal with a waterproof mastic or concrete mortar setting bed. The plastic resin we speak of using to make the translucent mosaics is weatherproof and especially elegant around water—fountains, screens at a swimming pool, or poolside tables are ideas you might like to develop.

There is a wide choice of projects for out-of-door use. Make table and bench tops, birdbaths, compass stones and paving blocks. Outdoor panels can be attached to gates and fences or built in as part of the structure. If the fence encloses a furnished area of the garden you will have an outdoor living room to furnish and this will give lots of opportunities for decorative effects.

Outdoor benches and counter tops for the barbeque area are good spots for mosaic, as is the fascia of the outdoor fireplace. Nameplates and house numbers make small, highly individual projects.

Small garden sculptures are fun to do. Instead of sawing outline silhouettes from wood and surfacing them, cast similar forms in lightweight concrete. To do this, scrape a place on the hard ground in some out-of-the-way spot in the garden and sketch a simple outline of a bird or fish, for instance. Then drive short stakes so they support 2″ wide strips of linoleum to follow your outline. Fill your form half full of concrete, then add wire mesh reinforcing and complete filling form with concrete. The next day, remove linoleum form and round edges. Handle very carefully at this point—let concrete set at least a week before handling it further. Then you can surface it with tiles or pebbles.

Pebbles on stepping stones laid in gravel walks or in larger paving areas are one of the pleasantest forms of outdoor mosaic. They seem perfectly natural underfoot, of course, and not only enrich concrete surfaces, they cut down glare and make quiet, undemanding decoration.

If you are lucky enough to have a garden and an interest in mosaic making, you'll not lack for interesting projects. Here are a few we have made for our garden.

compass stone

Set in a walk or entry way, this directional marker answers the question "Where's North?" at a glance. Choose the location first, then lay down a sheet of paper and rule North-South line as indicated on a compass. Our stone is set in a 16″ square angle iron form, 2″ deep; mosaic material is Venetian glass tile. Tile colors are two shades of green and blue-green and arrow point is bright red. Circle and arrow point are outlined in brass strip.

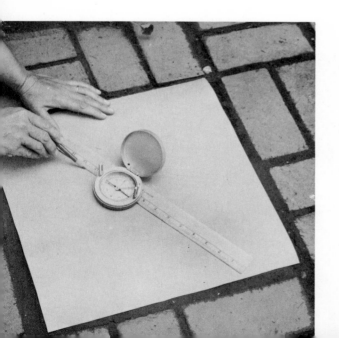

display disk for plants

A collection of succulents looks special displayed on this disk of concrete mortar set with vari-colored pebbles. Circle is based on an old washing machine lid—divisions are outlined with lead strips. Each pie-shape wedge is filled with pebbles of a single color—dark red, black, white and grey. Set this display disk on the ground or on a low stand as you please. Use it to show off potted plants as they look their best.

patio table

This table is 20″ x 20″, framed in angle iron and it stands 15″ high on angle iron legs. Lead strips laid on the plywood base held in the frame make the division lines in the pattern. The center section has yellow stones set in mortar colored with yellow ochre, sections on either side of this are surfaced with dark red stones set in mortar colored with burnt umber. Outer sections have brown-grey pebbles set in matching mortar made by mixing lampblack and burnt umber. Corners are gunmetal—black stones set in mortar colored with lampblack.

tile squares

These 9″ squares made up of scrap ceramic tiles mark the corners of the border on a reflecting pool in our garden. You'll find lots of uses for these simple designs. The bases for these tiles are 2″ reinforced concrete slabs. Mosaic was set in fresh mortar by the reverse method.

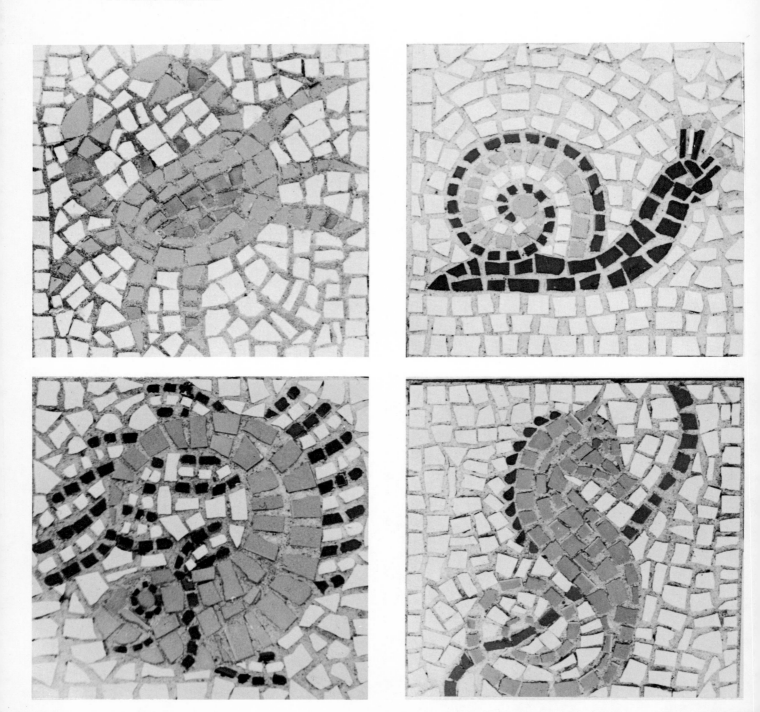

wood panel

This panel is entirely made up of weathered wood blocks cut from salvaged wood—some of it silvered after years of exposure. The panel is 4'2" x 14", framed in dull black finished wood. Colors are the natural ones of the various weathered woods—grey-browns, yellow-browns, red-browns, light silver grey and near-black. It has an architectural feeling that will make this, and similar panels, at home in an outdoor setting.

owl

This bird should perch on a porch, or some semi-protected spot as the pebbles are set in spackle on a plywood base sawed to a simple owl-shape. A large spool nailed to the plywood form makes a hanger that allows the owl to stand away from the wall and cast an interesting shadow on it. Our owl has deep shells for eyes, black pebbles for feathers and small round red ones for the speckles on his breast.

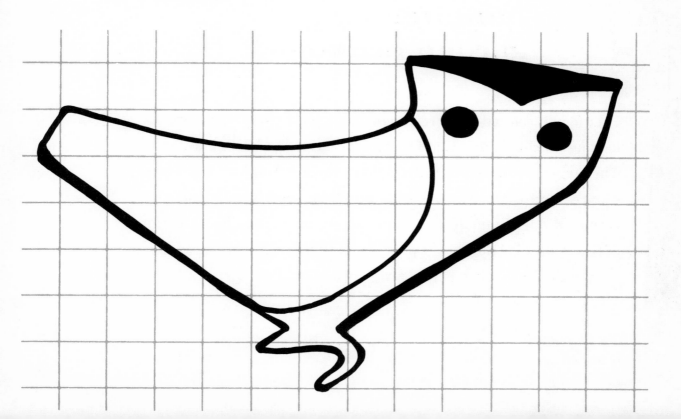

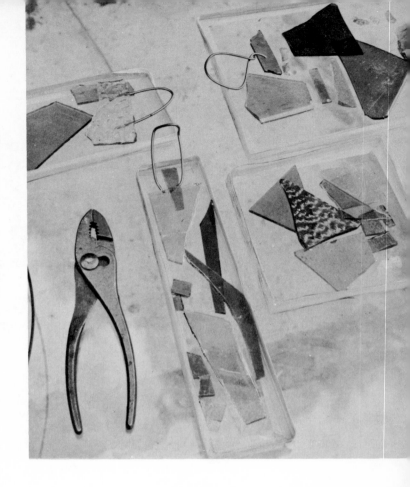

hanging
garden ornament

Plastic and colored glass rectangles hang and sway in the breeze, looking much like a strand from an Oriental wind bell, giant-size. The largest rectangle in the hanging ornament shown is about 8″ square. Scraps of stained glass are laid on sheet plastic and are then embedded in liquid plastic just as shown on page 25. A length of brass wire is laid in each panel before plastic is poured to make connecting links when panels are joined.

marine

The lobster and crab motifs used on this panel were put together with pieces of broken bottle glass—lobster is brown and the crab emerald green. None of the glass was cut. It was chosen from a large amount of broken, tumbled glass and assembled on the plastic backing panel jig-saw fashion. Plastic resin was poured around, but not over, these glass pieces and "sand" made by crushing glass was sprinkled over the background before the plastic set.

stepping stones

The forms for these stepping stones are made in a quick, easy way and the resulting shape is most pleasing. A center rib, 2″ wide and 20½″ long goes down the center of the form and remains in the stone. Outside walls of the form are 2″ strips of linoleum 25″ long. Tack or clamp an end of the linoleum strip to each side of rib ends. Fill half full with concrete mix. Place a section of reinforcing mesh on either side of rib—this board should have nails driven in it part way on either side to hold it in concrete—and fill the rest of the form with concrete mortar. This layer of mortar is the setting bed for the pebbles which are laid in stripes to resemble veins of a leaf. When concrete is hard, brush pebbled surface and remove the linoleum.

*Children are fascinated with mosaic making.
Let them set their "treasures" of stone and
shell and bits of wood in spackle.*

mosaic
for children

Children take to mosaic making as naturally as they do to turning out mud pies. If you put rock "raisins" in your mud pies as a child you'll recognize a similarity in technique! Even quite small children enjoy pushing the larger seeds and seed pods in a layer of soft clay or spackle.

Mosaics that children make needn't be permanent or practical — the experience in making them is the valuable part. The getting acquainted with the world of things around them and the developing of skills means more here than the completed object.

The work of artistic creation is a justifiable activity for anyone but is of greatest importance for children. Happily, most modern parents realize the desirability of providing the opportunities for individual creative expression.

Young children will be satisfied with an old baking pan with a layer of mixed spackle in the bottom of it and a collection of pebbles and shells. Some children like to make their own round-ups of mosaic material and will gather wood beads, jacks and old keys, etc. Almost any boy could make an interesting mosaic with the collection of things in his pockets!

Texture and variety are achieved by children more readily than pattern or design and necessity for the latter should never be imposed on them. As with painting, modeling and such forms of child art, it is best to let the child explore and invent and develop skills. So don't judge a child's work according to adult standards.

Naturally children mustn't be exposed to harmful materials— mortars or glues with chemicals that might get in the eyes or hair or glass with sharp edges, pointed tools, etc. This is why pebbles, shells, bits of driftwood, pods and large seeds, and other natural units that won't need cutting or breaking are recommended. Glass that has been tumbled to grind down sharp edges or melted to make glass pebbles is colorful, safe and of much interest to most children.

You could also provide small children with already cut rectangles of scrap linoleum. Older children can cut this material themselves and will like doing it. Children take joy in what really amounts to acts of destruction, although done for a constructive purpose, in smashing and breaking crockery and bottles. Such activity must be supervised, of course; bottles wrapped in layers of paper bags and plates put inside old magazines. Use your own judgment about this—you may not want to introduce the subject at all . . . Interest as well as abilities vary from child to child. The best way to interest a child in mosaic making is to be engaged in the work yourself. Children often love to handle mosaic materials and will divide and sort them as your "helper." If you've ever sorted a lot of pebbles you'll readily admit that help on this job can be most welcome, too.

Teen-agers will have strength and skill to permit use of any of the mosaic materials but find quick, satisfying results with colorful, easy-to-handle linoleum.

Teen-agers will sometimes bestir themselves to make gifts for others given incentive and opportunity. This is a wholesome attempt to be grown up, so encourage it. Linoleum is a good material here because it is colorful, easy to handle and will give quick and effective results. Glazed tiles are also satisfying if the project isn't too large to be completed before interest falters.

In mosaic making, as in other fields of human endeavor, interest grows with doing, satisfaction increases as skills grow. Help your children grow by giving them a chance to undertake interesting, skill developing activities. Mosaic making is one of these.

in conclusion

We believe that this book will tell you all that you will need to know to make your first mosaics. We also think that it will serve to increase your interest in mosaics. As this interest grows, you will enjoy seeking out more elaborate, advanced examples than we have presented here for beginning projects. Mosaics may be seen all around you. Today they decorate many private and public buildings. Smaller panels are often for sale in art galleries and in the shops that specialize in original decorative accessories for the home.

You may also want to look at old mosaics. A few museums have examples of ancient and medieval mosaics. Some you will find pictured in books. Ask a librarian at any large library to help you find books on Roman, Early Christian and Byzantine mosaics. These ancient mosaics will repay the most careful study.